MANAGING FAMILY FINANCES
for Career Couples

EPHRAIM UNUIGBE

MANAGING FAMILY FINANCES

for Career Couples

EPHRAIM UNUIGBE (ACA)

Copyright 2022 © **Ephraim Unuigbe**

ISBN - 9798842031818

All rights reserved.

No part of this book may be reproduced, distributed, stored, or transmitted in any form or by any means, including electronic, photocopy, recording, reproducing or resale without the prior written permission of the author and publisher, except in the case of brief quotations embodied in reviews and articles as well as certain other non-commercial uses permitted by copyright law.

Contact the author via info@ephraim-unuigbe.online

DEDICATION

I dedicate this book to every married couple out there working hard to make their relationship work.

TABLE OF CONTENTS

Dedication

Preface

Chapter 1: The Family..8

Chapter 2: Understanding Money....................................28

Chapter 3: To Combine or Not to Combine........................43

Chapter 4: Insurance and The Family................................58

Chapter 5: Children finance..70

Chapter 6: Panning for Retirement...................................83

Chapter 7: Dealing with Family Financial Emergencies.........95

About The Book..106

About The Author...107

Acknowledgments..108

Other Books by the Author to date.............................109

Services We Offer..110

Preface

This book seeks to provide guidance to working professionals on how to navigate their relationship finances while pursuing their career goals. It can be a challenge for new and young couples, especially in the beginning. It is true that not every couple fights over money, but for those who fight, there are techniques that can be employed to prevent such conflict in the future.

As I explain in this book, there are several very important aspects of the ideal family, and I provide an explanation of what each party brings to the table. The importance of setting a budget and how to adhere to it is also discussed. This book discusses the importance of speaking up and having a proper communication channel.

Having the right information is paramount to a happy family, and finances play a major role in a successful relationship. This book begins by discussing the importance of family and the duties and responsibilities of the two most important members of the family - the male and female. Furthermore, you will benefit from explanations regarding the finances of children, the benefits of insurance and how to take advantage of them, as well as proper retirement planning.

Money arguments are the second most common cause of divorce in the United States and are nearly as prevalent in other countries. In the UK, money worries are the leading cause of divorce, according to a survey.

I am confident that it will be a valuable resource for couples, especially young professionals as they navigate their career and family life.

Chapter One

-

The Family

The Family

The typical family consists of a man and a woman, followed by children at some point in time. It is this type of family that is referred to as the nuclear family. In addition to the man, wife, and children, there is an extended family made up of other individuals such as the mother, father, sister, brother, cousin, nephew, niece, etc. The term extended family is used to describe this category. While this book focuses on the financial management of a nuclear family, it is likely that the extended family will have some impact on the financial management of the nuclear family.

There are many variations of nuclear families these days, including the man with another man (homosexuals) and the woman and another woman (lesbians). In both cases, whether there are children or not. The following paragraphs explain why the other variants may not be ideal in a family context. The reason for this is that each member of the family - a man and a woman - have distinct duties and responsibilities that must be performed in order for the family to be successful.

These duties and responsibilities are not in any way related to chores or who pays what bills or whatever else you might have in mind. I am referring to duties and responsibilities that are more innate than physical in nature. There is something in the makeup of the individual, both as a man and as a woman.

This is why a man-man home, or a woman-woman home won't work well because of this. I would like to make it clear that this isn't just about finance or money, it's also about many other aspects of their lives, like how they raise their children, how they make decisions in the house, how they interact with each other and so on. Families are not supposed to be one-sided (man-man or woman-woman) in their original design. Neither as a single father nor as a single mother nor as two mothers nor as two fathers. It is my belief that, in terms of raising children, there will still be issues, even when both parties (man-man or woman-woman) give their best effort to the child or children.

A man is able to impart an expression to his son or daughter that two women cannot, as well as a unique characteristic that only a woman is able to impart to her daughter or son that two men cannot. You will have observed these deficiencies in our society among children from homes with parents of the same sex. It is not just my opinion; you can find research that has been conducted that supports this claim on the internet. It is the same for a single parent raising a family.

It is also for this reason that single parents are encouraged to remarry in order to provide their children with a more rounded upbringing, particularly when the children are still young - between the ages of 0 and 17 years. A child is only fully formed after this stage and would need the guidance of both his or her male and female parents in order to become a fully rounded individual.

This is not to suggest that children from these homes are unlikely to succeed in life or that any deficiencies they may have cannot be remedied. There are many examples of these children performing even better than children raised by parents of opposite sex.

This is only suggested to provide a wholesome childhood so that the children are able to develop the unique qualities from both parents as a result of the wholesome upbringing provided by both parents (a male and a female). It goes without saying that both members of a family must play their role in order to achieve the best results in an ideal family environment.

Even though this is not a book about marriage and family counselling, it is important for you to have a basic understanding of the concept of a family before delving into financial management. As an aside, if you know someone or you yourself were raised in a family that was not ideal as I mentioned above, the first step to healing from whatever negative traits or habits you may be experiencing is self-awareness. You can then begin to develop appropriate solutions or training to help you correct any of the character traits I mentioned earlier in your life.

The Man and His Characteristics in The Home

In a family, a man is the primary male figure and is intrinsically responsible for providing security for his wife and children. Additionally, he serves as a symbol of authority in the home. As a result of his presence at home, everyone in the household feels a sense of security and confidence. A man brings to the home a special kind of energy that only a man - the man of the house - can provide.

The fact that he is an active or inactive man does not matter, although the difference will be more obvious if he is an active husband and father. It does not matter whether he is an alpha male or not, that does not matter either. It is his presence that brings reassurance, comfort, confidence, protection, and some degree of relief to the house.

These advantages are missing in homes without men, which is why it is almost impossible to imagine a home without a man. In these homes, generally you will find a lack of order and direction, a lack of discipline, and a lack of confidence masked by arrogance. Consider, for instance, the lives of families without father figures in their homes to see what is being explained here if you are honest. There is a possibility that some of the children have now grown and no longer exhibit these traits outwardly, but deep down and especially if you are close to them, you will be able to see some of these traits.

Those characteristics that I mention are not simply what I have observed in others, but also what I have observed in myself since I was raised mostly by a single parent until the age of sixteen. I have since made a more conscious effort to correct them to become a better person as well as to ensure that they are not passed on to my children.

The Woman and Her Duties in The Home

The woman has a natural ability to manage and organize. She possesses a high level of confidence in this area. As a resourceful and productive person, she is a powerful agent of productivity. The popular explanation of one of my mentors, Myles Munroe, is that if you give a woman groceries, she will give you a meal, if you give her a seed, she will give you a child, if you give her a house, she will give you a home, and if you give her trouble, she will give it back to you in multiple fold. Whatever she receives, she multiplies.

A woman has an affectionate side that can only be expressed by her. She ensures that the home is in a state of balance. She commands calmness and peace with her gentleness and feminine presence.

It is her ability to connect the dots that are missing within a home that makes her powerful. In the Bible, there is a popular verse that states that he who finds a wife finds a good thing. Yes, it is true.

It is impossible for a man to be completely satisfied without a woman in his life. Men who succeed today without women by their sides are likely performing below their potentials. The problem with women only arises when a woman is not treated correctly by her husband, and when her emotions are not managed appropriately.

Women are multi-talented and capable of multitasking, unlike men. The potential of a woman is unlimited. She can be whatever she wishes without a great deal of effort. She is capable of making seemingly impossible situations possible when given the right environment.

You will often hear that behind every successful man there is a woman. I totally agree with this statement. It is most often the case that the man shines because there is a woman at his back cheering him on and providing him with the necessary nutrients. It is important to note that the nutrients here are not limited to physical nutrients, but also include mental, emotional, and spiritual nutrients.

Last but not least, it is important to observe what happens immediately following childbirth in order to gain a better understanding of the role of the mother in the life of her children. Children receive all their physical nourishment from their mothers until they are able to consume solid foods. You may have also noticed that a child stops crying when the mother carries the child. The child is soothed by her, and the woman is emotionally attached to the child not just then, but throughout the remainder of her life. The situation is different with the man. As a mother, she understands her children's emotions and she can connect with them more deeply than the man.

It is also common for a woman to serve as the resident doctor of her own home. Her knowledge of the needs of each member of her family is extensive. A woman completes the package.

The Needs of The Man and The Women

As I will be writing a separate book on this subject soon, I will not bore you with too much information about a man and a woman. I will simply provide a high-level overview. I believe this is an important aspect to consider giving you a sense of how each gender desires to be treated.

- The man needs (not wants) sex, while the female needs affection. There are times when a woman does not necessarily want sex, she may just wish to be held and cosy around you, which is interpreted by men as indicating that she desires sexual contact.

- The man is possessive, whereas the woman needs protection. It is due to the possessive nature of the man that they find it difficult to forgive their cheating spouse. Women need protection, which is why they want to be taken care of even if they earn more than their male counterparts.

- Having a conversation is essential for a woman, and having an attractive woman is essential for a man. It's highly likely that if a woman comes to you with her challenges, she does not want to hear about possible solutions. She just wants to talk to you. It is the conversation that attracts them and while they are having those conversations, they often get the solutions to the issues themselves. In contrast, the man is attracted to what he sees. Providing men with what they desire to see meets a core need since men are primarily visual beings.

- Honesty and openness are required by women, while domestic pleasure and support are required by men. This is what the man refers to as peace of mind.

- A woman needs financial support. The fact that they earn more than the man does not matter. Security is the sole driving force behind this need. It is the nature of women to receive and the nature of men to give. There is always a desire in a man to give. The true man finds fulfilment in giving, particularly to his spouse.

- Respect and admiration are essential for a man. Family commitment is essential for a woman. The man needs encouragement and praise as they serve as food for his ego. Women who understand this will be able to solve half of their domestic problems. By nagging him, you will only drive him to seek comfort with his "friends". On the other hand, the woman requires family commitment, or more simply, TRUST.

There is a need for her to be reassured that the man is in for the long haul. It is a dangerous thing to cause doubt in a woman's mind that you may not be in it for the long run. An important aspect of a woman's desire for family commitment is the way in which her husband treats her children. Having a good relationship with them and treating them right is important to her. She clearly desires that he serve as an example for them.

- The qualities that a woman needs are kindness, patience, understanding, empathy, and compassion. Women are more likely to require these than men, even though this is a requirement for both genders.

Bringing it All Together

Consider the attributes of both a man and a woman and decide whether a man-man home will be able to complement the strengths of either gender, as well as whether a woman-woman home will be able to provide a complete ingredient for a successful marriage and child-upbringing experience. It is important to note that opposite sex unions are not only about what they contribute to the children, but also about what they contribute to themselves. The two complement each other. An area of weakness in one is an area of strength in the other.

This chapter aims to provide you with a better understanding of the family and the roles each member of the family is expected to play. As a matter of fact, I understand it is possible that a mother may not be available in some cases for a number of reasons, such as when she does not make it during childbirth or if the father is in prison. While these are not ideal situations, it is important to try to find other positive alternatives owing to the many benefits of having a mother and father in the family.

It is important to note once again that this book is intended for the working couple, thus its focus. Additionally, I believe that this book answers the question, "what do you bring to the table?" through the explanations.

My Thoughts on Prenuptial Agreement

Generally, this is an agreement made by a couple before they marry concerning ownership of their respective assets in the event that the marriage ends in divorce. While this may appear to be a reasonable and necessary safeguard, I believe that it is totally pointless. It is like planning to fail before embarking on a journey. Prenuptial agreements should be drafted entirely in the name of the woman if they are going to be drafted at all. This provides her with the security she needs and settles her mind.

I believe that when a woman knows that her husband is putting all his eggs into one basket, and that the basket belongs to her, she will be committed to her family. In my opinion, if someone believes otherwise, they should not be getting married in the first place since marriage is for better or for worse and it is worth losing everything for the woman if it ends. A prenuptial agreement is a breeding ground for distrust.

Although it is true that the issues raised here regarding the needs of both genders and my view on prenuptial agreements are not exhaustive and may need to be considered individually in some cases, most people will be able to relate to them.

Bonus information – How to find a spouse

- Get to know people first before trying to marry them.
- Go with the right motive. Why do you want to be in a relationship?
- Use your network – you know good people, ask them for referral
- Use dating apps – be available and appear to be available so that people will reach out to you
- Go on dates in the open – Be wise while you are out there

- Be open minded – don't only rely on your list for the ideal man/woman

- Do you really want or need a spouse?

Chapter One Summary

- There is no doubt that the family is the most important unit of a nation. It has the potential to make or break the world.

- Marriage is primarily a partnership between a man and a woman

- Family members each bring something unique to the table, and they are all special

- The family relationship is not one of competition, but of collaboration.

- There is no need for prenuptial agreements in a marriage relationship

Chapter Two - Understanding Money

Understanding Money

Money is one of the most important things you will ever need in your lifetime. There is nothing wrong with wanting money and dreaming of having a lot of it. Quite the contrary, it is detrimental to not think about money and how to make a lot of it. There is only one thing that is evil, and that is the love of it. It is loving it when you attempt to acquire it by any means necessary, including cheating others or making use of illegal means.

Money is a means of exchange of goods and services. It is important that you note that I used the term a means of exchange and not the means of exchange because there are other ways in which you can exchange goods and services. There are a lot of other means for exchange, such as relationships, value creation, time, the environment, ideas, and so on.

In economics, there are three main reasons for holding money: they are for transactional purposes, for speculative purposes, and for precautionary purposes.

The Transactional Purpose for Holding Money

A person holds money so that he or she can spend it on physiological needs such as food, shelter, and clothing. The food you eat, the place you live, and the clothing you wear make up your lifestyle. It is for this reason that we hold money as a basic necessity. In order to facilitate transactions.

Money for Speculations

There are some people who do not understand why saving is important. It is important to save many times so that you may take advantage of opportunities as they arise from time to time. In much the same way that a bad clock is right twice a day, so too are opportunities. Regardless of whether you are expecting them or not, they will arrive. It is better to be prepared with your savings in order to take advantage of sudden opportunities rather than not be prepared and regret not doing so.

Precautionary Reason for Holding Money

There is no certainty about the future, at least not completely. Humans are not designed to see into the future. To predict what is likely to happen, they can only make inferences based on past and present information. As a result of this limitation, we plan. As a precaution, we plan for the "just in case". Emergencies do occur, whether it is a punctured tyre, a malfunctioning heater, or a sickness (in countries where healthcare is not free). It is important to keep in mind, however, that we keep and must use money to handle these emergencies in order not to worry about the future or become bankrupt. There is a dedicated chapter in my book that discusses the need for insurance - chapter 4.

Managing Money

Management of money involves ensuring that you are able to obtain what you desire, when you desire it, from the resources you have at your disposal.

The importance of this can never be overstated, since no amount of money can ever be sufficient. When you look around, you will notice that those who are considered rich are still seeking ways to improve their wealth. Have you ever wondered why the richest people in the world continue to work? It's not just because they are pleased with their job, although this may be a contributing factor. In most cases, it is due to the fact that they receive more money. Because money is a reward of value, individuals get excited when they receive rewards for their hard work.

Having realized that no amount of money will satisfy you, you must develop a plan to ensure that the "little" you have is managed adequately to meet your needs as well as those around you. The term "budget" is used in economics to describe this type of plan.

Basically, a budget is a financial plan that shows how much income you earn and how much you spend each period. The period can be weekly, monthly or even yearly. Your budget income should include the total amount; this includes all income you receive in cash or through bank transfers from work, including investment income, side income, gifts, bonuses and what some people may refer to as "free money." No, free money does not exist. It may be money that you did not plan for, but it is not free. Conversely, be generous enough to include everything you spend money on as an expense. Expenses should include everything from minor expenses such as gym memberships to major expenditures such as vacation planning. This is particularly important for those who are not yet familiar with budgeting and who are prepared to track all incomes and expenses.

You can find a variety of free budget templates on the internet that you can use to create a budget that works for your particular needs. Be careful, however, that you get one from a verified website to avoid being hacked so that you do not have to deal with security issues.

Sticking to a budget even when it is not convenient is the key to budgeting and using budgeting tools. It may be difficult at first, but eventually you will become accustomed to it and become more consistent. Make your budgeting approach innovative, such as using your smartphone to capture expenses as they occur so that you do not miss them, and transfer them to your template when you have a chance to do so. To be consistent, you will need to exert deliberate efforts and discipline. Like everything else in life, perfection can be improved through practice.

In my previous book - Let's Talk About Money - I provide information about managing money. Although it was written for those just beginning their careers and young professionals, some of the information will be of great value to you as well.

How to Make You Budget Work for You

In regard to budgeting, there is a general rule that I am going to share below, the 50/30/20 rule. In any case, what's important is that it is tailored to suit your individual needs. As far as this is concerned, there is no universal rule, and you are not required to strictly adhere to it if it does not suit or serve your needs. You may be able to make it a 20/30/50 or 10/10/80 or 20/10/70, for example. Essentially, there is no rigidity involved. You will find some more useful information about how to stick to a budget in chapter 7 of this book, but for now:

- Know your monthly income and expense (or weekly income if you earn weekly)
- Use the 50/30/20 rule as a simple budgeting framework.
    - Allow up to 50% of your income for needs.
    - Leave 30% of your income for wants.
    - Commit 20% of your income to savings and debt repayment.
- Monitor your budget on a regular basis.
- Be flexible with your plan
- Give yourself time to get used to it.

Investment

A person cannot save until he or she becomes wealthy. Investments are the most reliable means of creating wealth. It is highly unlikely that you will become wealthy by saving money. It is only through the investment of your saved funds that you can become wealthy. There are many people who make the mistake of believing that the more they earn and save, the richer they will become. This is one wrong way of thinking. If you have saved up money, you should invest it in investments that are reliable. That brings us to the next critical question - where should I invest my savings when I have accumulated a certain amount?

The majority of the time, I do not provide advice regarding where to invest their money. This is something that you can ask your accountant to assist you with. A number of factors must be taken into consideration when deciding on the best investment for you. This is why giving a blanket recommendation without understanding your particular situation, such as what you make, what you spend, your level of risk appetite, and so on, is often incorrect.

People tend to shy away from accepting the truth that higher risk results in higher returns. The principle is universal. When you are willing to invest your savings in a riskier investment, you are expected to earn higher returns and it is the same if you choose to invest in a less risky investment, the expected returns will be low.

One of my favourite investment tips is to avoid investing in investments that you are unfamiliar with.

I would also suggest that you invest your money in the stock market through Index Funds or Exchange Traded Funds (ETF) if you are looking for a more diversified approach to investing. Generally, these two investment pots provide good returns over the long term because they are well-diversified. My understanding is that Index Funds or ETFs provide a return of between 8 and 10% per annum over the long term. However, this investment should only be made for long-term investment purposes and should not be made for short-term or emergency purposes. A long-term investment should not be less than ten years.

Exchange-traded funds (ETFs) have become one of the most popular investment trends. These funds provide investors with a convenient method for accessing global stock markets without the need for significant investment experience. This application functions in the same way as a playlist, which includes the best songs, in this case, the top 500 or 250 shares. The majority of ETFs are linked to major indices such as the FTSE All Share or the S&P 500. Recent data indicates that the value of ETF assets exceeded $10 trillion by the end of 2021, according to various sources.

Before making a decision for yourself or your family, it is recommended that you consult with a competent investment advisor. Fortunately, this information is available online for free to anyone.

Investments that promise unrealistic returns
I have seen many young people and even individuals who would normally be expected to know better fall for the same trick regarding investments that promise quick wealth. Many parts of the world are experiencing hardship, resulting in the popularity of these schemes.

For the avoidance of doubt, if it seems too good to be true, it probably is. Investing works according to a natural law - the higher the return, the greater the risk. Essentially, this means that you are more likely to lose your money if you invest in investments that promise high returns. The reverse is also true - the lower the returns, the greater the chance that you will get back some interests from your investment.

How to Have the Right Money Mindset

- Decide to be financially successful
- Determine your life values
- Decide how much is enough
- Be open minded about money
- Find ways to be content
- Obtain the training you require
- Forgive your past financial mistakes

Chapter Two Summary

- The higher the return, the greater the risk.

- Engage a professional accountant or investment advisor before making investment.

- If it seems too good to be true, it probably is.

- Don't invest in what you do not understand.

- You need to have the right mindset about money.

Chapter Three - To Combine or Not to Combine

To Combine or Not to Combine

In chapter one - The family, we summarized all the characteristics of the two important people in a marriage - the man and the woman. It is necessary to think about whether to combine or not to combine in order to succeed in that union.

The truth is that there is no right or wrong answer to this question, but the final resolution depends on the circumstances of the home, and the situation of the home can be very different from one family to the next. In order to help you make a more informed judgment for what is right for you, we will examine the different options available to us to help you choose the best one

Factors to consider when deciding whether to combine

When deciding whether to combine or not, there are a number of factors that must be taken into consideration. Throughout the next few paragraphs, we will be taking a closer look at these points in a critical manner.

- **Open conversation**

    Communication is a powerful tool, and I believe it to be a superpower. In most cases, people neglect this superpower, especially when it comes to family situations. It is important to realize that a lot of the things you encounter in this life are out of your control.

    There are many factors beyond your control, things you cannot even predict. For instance, you cannot be a solely responsible for who the president of your country will be, you cannot predict whether World War 4 will happen, you cannot tell if you will be offered a promotion in your career next year, even if you have been promised, but you can somehow influence what is going on in your home just by having a simple conversation with your family members.

The best thing to do is to have a conversation about all the things that are bothering you (not nagging) and come up with something that will resolve it immediately. The truth is that the more money conversations you have, the more the other party will be able to understand how honest you are and how strongly you believe in the relationship. In this way, you can gain a better understanding of what each party wants from the other and what their expectations are regarding the handling of money.

I have observed that many people simply wait and suffer in silence instead. There is a tendency for most people to wait for something to happen, perhaps an external force to be the trigger for an upward spiral. Perhaps some miracle will occur. Others are waiting for someone else to initiate the action that will change their own lives. Every aspect of life requires that you be able to speak up about your feelings, pass information, and assert your rights. Even though it may seem easy, many people do not take advantage of this ability. You can demand anything you wish at work if you feel that you have earned it. As long as you are entitled to it, you may demand anything at all you wish.

- **Defining boundaries**

There are some people who wish to have their own space, and this is perfectly acceptable. In this case, communication is essential. A spouse may wish to have some control over their finances. They should be able to exercise that control. There are some people who are wired differently, and having control gives them some sense of security.

While boundaries are important, they do not imply that the spouse is not responsible for his or her obligations within the family. There will still be a need for them to fulfil their part of the family obligation, as well as maintaining the boundaries that they require.

Even before getting married, it is important to discuss this topic. Nevertheless, if this was missed initially and it is causing a problem now, please allow them to have that boundary.

- **Who is responsible for what?**
On the list of things to do, this should be at the top. It is very important to set a goal from the beginning, especially in a family, so that everyone knows that they are responsible for the achievement of the goal. Is it the man's responsibility to pay rent while the woman's is to pay for groceries or vice versa?

Is it the woman's responsibility to plan and pay for the annual vacation and the man's responsibility to pay for the meal during the vacation? Is there a need for each individual to set aside some of their salary on a monthly basis to be able to meet significant expenses like buying a house in the future? Who will be responsible for what and to what extent will they be held responsible? These are some examples that can be discussed. As soon as all these factors are clearly defined from the start, it becomes easier for everyone involved to plan their own individual parts in advance.

- **Patterns of Spending**

    There is no doubt that this is a very important factor that needs to be considered before making such a vital decision. There are some individuals who are unreliable with money, and it would not be a good idea to put your family's money in their hands. It is important that you know yourself.

    In my previous book, How to Choose a Career Path, I have given a great deal of attention to self-awareness. If you are a party that is incapable of managing money and you are aware of it, I will recommend that you leave the money to the other party who is capable of doing so. It is important for you to be reasonable and acknowledge your limitations in this situation. You should allow the other party to handle it since you know they will be able to do a better job than you.

- **Financial history**

There is a possibility that one party may have had some financial obligations in the past in the form of student debt or some other commitments. As we said before, it is worth discussing what would work for both parties in order to find a solution. There may be a sense of contradiction when stating that past wealth (prenuptial agreements) should not be safeguarded, but debt should be taken into account as a possible safeguard. There is, however, a significant difference between the two. As a matter of fact, past debt discussion is just a matter of understanding how the other party perceives the situation from their perspective.

Love is lacking in a prenuptial agreement as it is only a bid to safeguard past wealth, but if you take the other person into account and discuss past debt, it shows you are considerate and care about them. Trying to force your past debt on the other party is not an act of love. The decision regarding whether to participate in past debt should be left to them.

To combine

What is the extent to which you wish to combine your finances, if you decide to do so? In order to avoid a party feeling cheated and to prevent any inconveniences from being caused to another party, please determine the percentage that would work for both of you. The important thing to remember is that this book is intended for couples who work together, which means that both the man and the woman are working. In the case of one person working, the answer is straightforward. A working party provides all the necessities for the family while the other party contributes in another way to the family.

In addition, it is important to note that the decision to combine or not to combine has nothing to do with love but rather with understanding. Having said that, let us consider the various options available to us. The process of combining can be divided into two general categories.

The full Approach

There is no separate account for each party in this case. There is a central account where all the funds are deposited, and everyone spends from there. As a result, family budgeting becomes easier, as well as transparency is enhanced. In contrast, if one person is a high spender and the other one is a frugal person, there could be an imbalance in their financial habits that can lead to resentment.

A practical example

In this example, party A earns £5,000 while party B earns £7,000. Both couple's earnings are deposited into a joint account, which is used to pay all the household bills every month.

In addition to this, the couple uses a joint credit or debit card to pay all their bills, regardless of whether it is a household bill such as a TV, or whether it's an individual purchase such as a new car.

The hybrid Approach

In this approach each party has their own accounts where their personal funds are deposited, and then there is a joint account in which the entire family obligation is deposited. It is important to note that the percentage of payment depends on the individual's earning ability and their agreement from the beginning. The joint account is used to pay for things such as rent or mortgage payments as well as bills.

A major advantage of maintaining this approach is that each party can maintain a degree of independence while jointly meeting family obligations. There is also the advantage that a party can purchase a surprise gift for the other party or incur other personal expenses without having to explain why.

In this case, the disadvantage occurs only if there is no agreement on how much each party should contribute to the joint purse. This can lead to resentment between the parties.

A practical example

The monthly incomes of Y and Z are respectively £6,000 and £4,000. The income of Y constitutes 60% of the household income, while the income of Z constitutes 40% of the household income. Each month, the couple spends £3,000 on their family's bills. A monthly bill of £3,000 is paid by Y in the amount of 60%, equivalent to £1,800, and by Z in the amount of 40%, equal to £1,200.

It is important to remember that the hybrid approach should be tweaked until everyone is satisfied with the results. Even though Y earns 60% of the household income, this does not imply that he must pay only 60% of the household expenses. As a matter of fact, he can actually pay even more or less, depending on Z's understanding and agreement. Compromise is an integral part of the marriage union. Be prepared to adjust your position if necessary.

Final Words

Consider your approach from a practical standpoint as much as possible. You may need to adjust the options available repeatedly until you find the one that is most appropriate. There is no universal formula for determining what works. It is probably not what you expected when you purchased the book, but there is simply no other way to look at it.

The book's motive is to help you explore the options available and learn what other families are doing to navigate this tricky slippery step. It was my intention to use a slippery step since money is one of the leading causes of separation. Take steps to ensure that your union does not fall into the wrong statistics by making it work for both of you.

Chapter Three Summary

- There is no right or wrong answer to whether to combine.

- Consider all the options available to you when you are having the conversation.

- There may be a need to define boundaries. It is okay.

- There is a need to consider financial history of your partner before deciding to combine.

- Be prepared to make adjustment and keep an open mind

Chapter Four

–

Insurance and The Family

Warning: Insurance discussions will involve morbid topics.

Insurance and The Family

The concept of insurance is one of the most misunderstood in the world, especially in developing countries. For instance, in developing countries, there is the belief that God will take care of every uncertainty, so there is no need to consider the insurance option. I agree that this may be true, but I believe that it is almost the height of irresponsibility. It is important to back up your beliefs with some actions. There is no question of doubt, but rather a matter of action supported by faith. It is a state of understanding that enhances your faith.

A person's mind will be much more relaxed and less anxious if he or she knows that as well as putting your faith in God, you have taken out an insurance policy that will energise that faith. It is this assurance that gives you the confidence that if you suffer a loss, you will be compensated. In spite of insurance, there have been instances when people have suffered losses without receiving compensation. Perhaps this is due to the fact that there are numerous technical explanations. However, this should not be interpreted as a reason for not taking out one.

In spite of the fact that insurance is more prevalent in developed countries, most people are unaware of the many benefits associated with it. Rich individuals are aware of this and take advantage of it to minimize their tax burden. The information about some insurance plans that you can take advantage of to reduce your tax liabilities is available on the internet for free or most times, you can speak to an insurance agent for free as well.

In light of the above description, it is essential that you grasp the concept of insurance so that you are able to fully appreciate the importance and ensure that you are taking the appropriate steps in order to reap the benefits.

A policy of insurance, according to a dictionary definition, is a contract through which a company or the government guarantees the payment of compensation for a specified loss, damage, illness, or death in exchange for a specified premium.

An alternative definition of insurance is that it provides protection against possible unforeseen events.

The first definition is more comprehensive and highlights two key characteristics of an insurance policy. In the first instance, it provides a guarantee, and in the second case, you are required to pay a premium. It is important to note that the guarantee is only valid if you pay your premium promptly and consistently as required by the contract.

As a family, you may choose from a number of insurance policies. From our definition, you may have noted that it can be for a specified loss, damage, illness, or death. In recent years, more and more people have taken out unemployment insurance.

Specified loss

In the business world, this has become quite popular among a lot of companies. A company takes out insurance policies in order to protect themselves from losses that may occur in the event of a disruption to its operations. Despite having an internal framework for dealing with uncertain situations, many businesses prefer to outsource risks in order to diversify their options.

As a means to diversify your options, you may consider obtaining an insurance policy for specified losses in your home or business.

Damage

"If you love anything in this life, insure it." is one of my favourite quotes. Consider your mobile phone as an example. If it falls off while you are holding it, you may lose vital information that may be contained therein. Despite the fact that there are other options available for protecting the contents, it does not prevent an individual from suffering from the emotional burden caused by the damage to their phone.

Again, whatever it is that you love, make sure you insure it. As a matter of fact, this is a wise thing to do.

Illness

It is impossible to predict illness, and it does not matter whether an individual leads a healthy lifestyle, exercises regularly, or consumes only vegetables as part of their diet. It does not matter whether an individual is rich or poor, sickness affects everyone alike.

It is important to note that sickness may have a greater impact on some people than others based on their circumstances. This can include the loss of a job, permanent disability, damage to a vital organ, among others. In order to minimize the impact of illness, it is wise to obtain health insurance. While considering sickness insurance, there are a number of options to consider, and I recommend that you speak with an insurance professional about your options. You should not assume that you have a complete understanding of what is required; you should seek professional advice.

Death

Here is the elephant in the room. Even though every individual will encounter it at least once, some even twice, nobody wants to speak about it. There are many things that humans do not have control over, and this is one of them. Although it may take longer than anticipated, it is inevitable in the end. Therefore, if it is known that we are all going to face this type of situation, why don't people take steps now to prepare for it?

Because death insurance is a certainty, it is also known as assurance. Insurance policies for life/death are available in various forms. There are a number of types of life insurance available, including term life insurance, whole life insurance, universal life insurance, variable life insurance, burial insurance/funeral insurance, survivorship life insurance/joint life insurance, mortgage life insurance, credit life insurance, etc.

An insurance agent can provide you with a more comprehensive understanding of the options available to you and your situation, as well as how to proceed.

The Importance Of Taking Out An Insurance Policy

- The future is uncertain
- It provides you with peace of mind
- You care about some people and wish to take care of them even if you are no longer physically or mentally able to do so
- This is a wise course of action, and you will be counted as part of the wise class
- Most countries require insurance as a matter of law

Risk

A discussion of insurance would be incomplete if risk was not discussed. The word - RISK has been mentioned several times in previous paragraphs of this chapter. By understanding what risk is, we will be able to better understand insurance and appreciate the value it offers.

My definition of risk is simply the possibility of damage or loss. The situation involves the possibility of danger. Everyone is exposed to danger at one point or another in their dealings, so it is important to have a backup plan in place in order to provide them with protection.

There is a possibility, and because that possibility exists, it is worthwhile to consider taking out a plan. At least to give you a sense of assurance that you are safe in any way.

In general, insurance can only cover three types of risks, which include liability risk, property risk, and personal risk. These are the risks that we have already discussed.

Several other risks are not insured by insurance companies. At the time of writing this book, uninsurable risks include reputational risk, regulatory risk, trade secret risk, political risk, and pandemic risk. In the future, it is possible that some insurance companies will be able to cover these other risks.

Lastly, I recommend that you seek professional advice from a local insurance broker for tailored advice based on your specific needs. This book does not constitute professional advice regarding investments or insurance. It is important that you speak with a competent professional who can provide you with specific advice based on your individual circumstances.

Chapter Four Summary

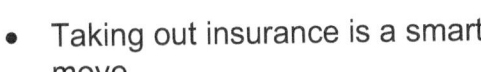

- Taking out insurance is a smart move.

- There are insurance policies you can take to reduce your tax obligations.

- The future cannot be predicted

- Not all risks can be insured.

- One advantage of insurance is peace of mind.

Chapter 5

—

Children Finance

Children Finance

The gift of a child or children is one of the greatest gifts of marriage. In some cases, our children follow the same career path as us, while in others, they pursue a different career path. Whichever way they choose, it is our responsibility to provide them with the right tools and resources in order for them to be successful. The right tools and resources do not necessarily have to be financial; they can simply take the form of communicating value to them and providing them with intangible gifts that will prove valuable to them in the future.

Consider your own life. Do you have any things that you wish you had known earlier that could have given you the edge? It is these things that you can give to your children now that will give them a head start in life. As I mentioned earlier, it doesn't have to be financial even though we are discussing finance for children in this chapter. It doesn't have to be about money.

To gain a better understanding of children's finances, it is imperative that you begin teaching them about money as early as possible. There is no specific age when you should begin, you can start whenever you perceive that they are able to comprehend. You should explain to them what money is in general and what it means to you. Make sure they understand the value of hard work and handiwork. Children should be taught the importance of giving something in exchange for money.

Educate them about the fact that money doesn't just appear out of nowhere. Make sure that they know there is no quick method of earning money. It is essential that they learn that true wealth can only be acquired by deliberate hard work, and that if they gain wealth by accident, there is a high probability that they will also lose it.

It is also important to teach them that, in life, there are some things that are more important than money. These include relationships, time, family, character, friendship, trust, integrity, and security, among others. It is important for them to learn the art of contentment because sometimes they will not receive everything they desire even if they make all the right decisions and follow all the right steps.

It is again important to emphasize that children can learn a great deal in their early years and will use that knowledge for the rest of their lives. Last but not least, teach all of these things by example. You are seen by children in a way that you cannot possibly comprehend or imagine. Children should not be taught exclusively in words in the hopes that words will be sufficient on their own, teach them by your lifestyle.

Children are observant and take note of things you may or not even be aware of. Our thoughts and values that we have ingrained in us allow us to do some things without consciously thinking about them, unintentionally, but the children see them. As a result, we must nourish our minds by reading good books, listening to people we respect - mentors, watching good movies, and listening to good music and so on.

When it comes to raising your children, there are some things you will need to sacrifice in order to instil the right behaviours in them. Although this is not a book about raising children, I thought it was important to lay the right foundation, so your children will not only have a solid financial advantage, but they will also have other important components to sustain that advantage.

Building a Financial Advantage for Your Children

As mentioned earlier, it is imperative that you teach your children about money, but I did not provide any information concerning the keys to making this happen. This section discusses some of the actions you can take.

- Savings - This is one key that is beneficial to both children as well as adults. The process of saving involves putting aside a portion of your income for the future. As we have discussed earlier, the three reasons for holding money are transactional, speculative, and precautionary. It is important that you set aside a portion of your personal savings for your child/children as well. Don't worry about the amount but remain consistent. Beginning early is the best way to ensure that they are well prepared for the future, as a small amount each month can go a long way. Making regular savings for your children should not be postponed until after you become a parent. It is important to begin as soon as you become aware of the need to do so.

As you save for your children, it is also important to teach them to save as well. Help them understand and save a portion of the money they receive from you or anyone else. This is also an excellent opportunity to explain why and how this is beneficial to them.

Although it is usually recommended that you open a separate account for your child or children, you may also wish to add their savings to your general savings account. The most important thing to bear in mind here is that a portion of the savings you are making will be used for your child.

If you make regular monthly savings of $50 and remain consistent for 18 years, you will have accumulated $10,800; $50 multiplied by 12 months in a year multiplied by 18 years. Consistent saving is what gives savings its power. As an illustration, your initial savings can be $100, or even $500 per month, depending on what you are able to do, and you will see the positive impact it will have in your children's lives.

- Investment - You will probably note from our example above that the savings of $10,800 in 18 months could have been more if it was better put into use - like. Earlier, I explained that you cannot save your money for wealth. From the example above, you will see that the savings of $10,800 could have been even greater if it had been utilized more effectively. As I explained earlier, one cannot save money in order to become wealthy. Having a method for multiplying your savings will assist you in overcoming one of the impediments associated with the time value of money - inflation. Investment is the vehicle for achieving this goal. When you make the right investment for your children, you can turn that $10,800 into as much as $20,000 through the power of compound interest at 8% per year.

Regardless of whether you understand this or not, don't just leave the money in a savings account. Investing in ETFs is the most efficient way to maximize the returns on your investment in shares. I have explained how in the previous chapter. The power of compound interest cannot be overstated. If you would like to learn more about compound interest, you can read online articles to get the most out of it. Additionally, you may need to consult with an investment advisor for the best investment based on your current circumstances and the future of your children.

- A home - Besides saving and putting money aside for investments for your children, one can also provide the gift of a home to them as a good financial investment. While I acknowledge that this may seem like an intimidating task, especially if you do not own one of your own, this is a worthwhile investment you can make for them, nonetheless.

Depending on where you live, you may start by purchasing a piece of land and then setting aside a certain amount of money every month to complete the construction. Whether you have completed the house or not, it will be a wonderful gift to give them when they reach adulthood. Having this advantage will give them an advantage when starting out in life.

There may be some form of taxation associated with this type of gift in some parts of the world. Before making such a decision, it is important to seek the advice of qualified professionals.

- Lead by example - It is unlikely that all of this will make any sense if you do not lead by example. If you do not practice what you teach, you cannot teach properly. The management of children's finances begins with you, the parents, and how you handle your finances.

Why not ask yourself? Would you be proud if your child handled money in the same manner as you do? It is then more logical to pass on your legacy to the next generation when you know that they are in good hands. These are the hands that you have trained yourself.

It is the responsibility of both parents to teach their children the importance of financial responsibility. There cannot be a situation where one is showing a good example, while the other is showing a completely different and contradictory example at the same time.

There is a need for you as parents to get serious about your financial responsibility, first of all towards yourselves, and then toward your children as well. There are a number of ways in which you can set an example for your children to follow.

- Pay your debt
- Teach them about money
- Invest as early as possible
- Have a college plan for them
- Take an insurance plan for them
- Set up a Will
- Show them what you are doing

Chapter Five Summary

- Leading by example cannot be overemphasized.

- Children should be taught the importance of giving something in exchange for money.

- Teach them that they must provide value to get money.

- Children are observant and take note of things you may or not even be aware of.

- Consider ways to give your children a financial head start in life.

Chapter 6

—

Planning for Retirement

Planning for Retirement

Retirement is perhaps one of the less discussed topics among young professionals. It is always assumed that one must reach a certain age before one begins to think about retirement. However, this could not be further from the truth. One of the most important questions you should ask as soon as you begin working is what your retirement plan is.

In addition to planning for savings, budgeting, investments, and all the other important money decisions you will be making, it is also important to plan for retirement. It is important to understand that planning for retirement does not imply that you will retire soon. The term merely indicates that somewhere in your mind you are aware that it is inevitable that you will need to retire at some point and that you are creating concrete plans to make sure you are able to retire comfortably.

Having a solid retirement plan is about knowing that you are comfortable when you retire and having everything you have as a working professional that you currently have when you retire. As with everything worth doing, retirement requires a lot of planning in order to make it a success.

Understanding what retirement is

The term "retirement" refers to the act of withdrawing from one's position or occupation or active working life. Alternatively, an individual may semi-retire by reducing their work hours or workload. It is common for people to retire when they become elderly or are unable to do their jobs due to health issues.

What retirement is not

A person may withdraw from a primary occupation while maintaining a less demanding or more relaxed occupation. It is not considered retirement, but rather a change of employment. When an individual leaves their employment with an organization to start their own small business, that is not considered retirement. Even if an individual is capable of working or is unable to work, he or she is not considered retired until he or she stops working.

Considering the above, it can be concluded that an individual can retire in a variety of ways, such as the traditional retirement - a complete withdrawal from work, the semi-retirement - a reduced workload or work hours or the temporary retirement - a career break.

It is important that you understand this difference so that you can plan accordingly. Not only in terms of financial planning, but also in terms of other essential aspects of retirement.

The traditional retirement method has become less and less feasible in today's society, even for those who have reached the age of retirement. The reason for this is not just the ability or inability to sustain a lifestyle at that age, but also the necessity for some active responsibilities in order to extend one's life span. The exception would be if the individual was totally incapacitated.

How To Prepare for Retirement

- **Savings**

Even though retirement is not solely about finances, it is important to understand that money will probably drive all other aspects of retirement. Later in this chapter, I will discuss these other aspects. Saving begins with determining how much income you will need in retirement. As soon as you gain an understanding of this concept, you will be able to determine how much money you need to set aside on a monthly or annual basis in order to achieve your goal.

Depending on your retirement needs, you will need to determine how much savings you might need. It is likely to assist you in determining whether you need to increase your contribution to your pension plan, or other retirement plans, or to earn additional income, or to learn about investment opportunities that can be exploited to your advantage.

- **Social Security benefits**

As important as it is to save for retirement, it is also important to understand what other social security benefits you are eligible for. There are some countries that provide retirement benefits to their citizens. While it will differ from country to country and the laws may have changed before you reach retirement age, it is still important to understand and plan accordingly.

In retirement, one can enjoy various benefits depending on their country of residence, including whether they are low-income earners, whether they are required to pay rent and bills, whether they can claim benefits, and if they are disabled.

- **Deal With Your Debts**

It is important to pay attention to debt as it may get overlooked in the journal when you focus on saving for the future instead of considering your current circumstances. You should consider getting rid of debt as part of your pre-retirement planning. There is a high probability that you will incur some liabilities during your working years, and you need to have a plan in place on how you intend to resolve those liabilities before you retire. It is not desirable to retire and still have debt to service.

The more important thing is to plan ahead, even if you cannot pay off your debt completely before retirement. Perhaps you should consult a debt adviser who can help you develop a budget and a repayment plan. Additionally, they will be able to provide you with advice regarding how to contact your creditors in order to arrange repayments. There are some organizations that may be able to assist you in negotiating with your creditors.

It is generally recommended to pay off your mortgage debt first, then your rent, and then your other debts in the order of priority. By paying off the mortgage, the individual is no longer at risk of becoming homeless, and other debts are easier to pay off.

- **Emotional Preparation**

A retirement can be a life-changing experience, and it can sometimes seem as if we have lost our identity as an individual after retirement. You can take comfort in the knowledge that everyone retires at some point in their lives. Consequently, you are not alone when it comes to retirement. It is equally as important to plan in advance as it is to have the right mindset.

I have outlined some ways in which you can prepare yourself emotionally for retirement.

- Plan in advance of what you will be doing.
- Take the time to consider what hobby or interest you would like to pursue.
- As your social circle shrinks after leaving employment, you should make new friends.
- Do something positive and put yourself out there
- Retirement is not a death sentence, so maintain a positive attitude and plan to make the most of your retirement years.

Retirement: 20 things to do

The following are some things you can plan for your retirement, and I believe that can help you start to view retirement positively.

- Consider mentoring youngsters
- Pursue another passion
- visit a new country
- Learn a new language
- Become a tour guide
- Join or start a community of retired folks like yourself.
- Start a book club
- Make art.
- Work on a business plan
- start a small business.
- Consider starting for a fun part-time job.
- Consider volunteering in your community
- Spend more time with family
- Research your family tree
- Travel to your favourite destination

- Nurture a hobby
- Consider a new adventure
- Keep your home clutter-free.
- Visit fun places
- Stay active, flexible, and vibrant

It is likely that you already have several ideas circulating in your mind. The most important thing to remember is that you are not alone. It may be necessary for you and your partner to perform these tasks independently or jointly, depending on the circumstances. There is no doubt that retirement can be an enjoyable experience and something to look forward to.

Chapter Six Summary

- Everyone will retire someday.

- Consider all the ways to prepare for retirement.

- There are fun things you can continue to do even at retirement.

- Retirement is not a death sentence.

- In addition to saving money, emotional preparation is an important aspect of retirement.

Chapter 7

—

Dealing with Family Financial Emergencies

Dealing With Family Financial Emergencies

The term "family emergency" refers to an event or situation that is beyond your control and cannot be prevented. The focus of this chapter is primarily on how to properly manage your finances as a couple when you are experiencing personal or other emergency situations, whether it is an extended family emergency, an emergency with a friend, or an emergency with other loved ones.

The majority of any personal family emergencies that may arise have been addressed in chapter 5 when we discussed insurance. However, we did not discuss how you are going to make provision for additional family emergencies that cannot be insured. This is due to the fact that not all risks can be transferred.

Additionally, this topic is particularly important for cultures where caring for extended family members is a big deal, and it can cause a lot of tension between couples in such cultures.

There has not really been much discussion in this book about how to budget for the family. There is no doubt that budgeting is one of the most important aspects of managing the finances of a family. The topic of budgeting prominently featured in my precious book - Let's talk about money - has been extensively discussed in the book. I understand that this is a personal perspective, but it will help couples make sense of it if you understand it from that perspective.

To summarize, budgeting is a method of setting aside a certain amount of money in a budget in order to meet a future need. In order to make sure that a future need can be met, it is necessary to know how much income the household has. Household income is all the money that comes into the family from a variety of sources, such as salary from a regular job, income from side jobs, or even investment income. To put it simply, it is a term that refers to all sources of income, whether they are earned or unearned. Having established that, it becomes much easier to plan for the various future needs that may arise once that has been established.

As a rule of thumb, you should always start your budget by paying yourself first. In spite of the fact that this may seem quite basic, it is often the case that many people pay for everything else before they think about themselves. There is no doubt that the amount of money you pay to yourself is a good indication of how valuable you think you are in your own eyes. Of course, this is going to depend a great deal on how much you earn in the first place. Having a job is not just a way to pay off your bills and to meet the needs of other people, but also for your own satisfaction. I believe this is important, but it isn't why you are working at all.

When it comes to budgeting, you (the wife and husband) are the most important factor. In other words, you are the goose that laid the golden eggs. If the goose is not well taken care of, then there will never be an egg to lay if that goose does not lay eggs. It is therefore imperative that you prioritise yourself in your budget. It will be easier for you to concentrate on the other aspects of the budget once you have a basic understanding of this. I think that a better way to understand this is to compare it with a message that the airline operators have been trying to communicate for many decades, but we still don't seem to get it. The message is "Put on your own oxygen mask before helping someone else".

You would have a better understanding of your circumstances and what may constitute an emergency in your family. Examples of emergencies include the premature birth of a baby, the loss of employment by a partner, an emergency car expense, an emergency home repair or expense, etc. You should allocate a budget for each of these items. In order to prepare for emergencies such as these, it is necessary to set aside a regular sum of money each month. Experts recommend that you save at least six months' worth of your monthly income for emergencies. In some cases, this may be higher or lower depending on where you live or/and your circumstances.

A portion of your budget may also be designated for charity, or if you prefer, a provision for others. Do not overshoot your charity budget in order to accommodate other people's "emergencies". It is important to remember that you are working with a budget, and that every cost has a purpose. In the event that you exceed your budget in any area, this could cause some level of inconvenience in other areas as well.

As I mentioned earlier, this is not a justification for being selfish or ungenerous, but rather a method of prioritizing. Identify the priorities - who matters most in the budget - you. Keep in mind that you are the one who lays the golden egg, and you deserve to be looked after. In the event that some flexibility is needed in the family budget, it should be agreed upon by both parties before any adjustments to accommodate others are made. The chapter three of this book - To combine or not to combine - contains an explanation of how flexibility can be applied. If you need a refresher on what you learned in that chapter, please refer to it again.

To assist you in creating a workable budget, I have highlighted some behaviours you may want to adopt. It is important to note that this list is not exhaustive.

How To Manage Your Spending

The following are some of my tips for staying within my budget. Also included in this consideration is whether or not what you should give to others and how much I should give.

- Compare brands – It is imperative that you do not simply make purchases on a brand without comparing it with other brands that may provide even better value and satisfaction. This is especially important when making a large purchase. You can obtain comparison information from several websites.

- Whenever you are making large purchases, take your time - you may want to sleep on the decision for a few days or even weeks before deciding whether this purchase is necessary. It is never a good idea to purchase on impulse, especially when it comes to large purchases.

- Review your subscriptions - it may be worthwhile to examine whether all of your subscriptions are still necessary. It is possible that you are spending money on unnecessary expenses. Does Netflix still meet your needs? How about Amazon Prime? Is it really necessary to subscribe to all these television channels?

- Consider how much you are willing to spend and how long it will take you to earn it at work. For example, if you earn £10 per hour and need to make a purchase of £500. It will take you 50 hours to complete this task. By doing so, you will be able to determine whether it is worthwhile

- Make sure you do not spend more than you have - this is a no-brainer. You should cut your coat according to the size of your clothes, not the size of your body.

- Make meal planning a part of your lifestyle. This here is a supersaver technique. You will always need food and if you are not careful, you may end up spending more than you expect. Proper planning helps you know when to eat out and when to eat in and again depending on what you earn, make eating in a habit.

- Others – Instead of using credit, use cash. Get rid of bad habits - you know what your bad habits are and keep an eye on your savings. Simply refraining from spending money is a very simple way to make money. In no way does this mean that you should suffer in any way as your money accumulates while you sit on it.

Chapter Seven Summary

- As some risks are not insurable, you must plan for them.

- Consider the many tips to manage your spending.

- Have a budget for charity to guide your giving to others.

- Consider paying yourself first in your budget.

- You are the goose that lay the golden eggs. So, take care of yourself first.

About the Book

Not all couples fight over money but for those who do, there are ways to prevent it.

The importance of finances in a successful relationship, and having the right information is paramount to a happy family, is something I strongly believe in. The first chapter of this book discusses the importance of the family as well as the duties and responsibilities of the two most important members of the family - the male and female.

Money arguments are the second most common cause of divorce in the United States and are nearly as prevalent in other countries. In the UK, money worries are the leading cause of divorce, according to a survey.

About The Author

Ephraim Unuigbe is a chartered accountant and a career and personal finance coach. The author holds a BSc in Accounting, as well as membership in the Institute of Chartered Accountants of Nigeria and certification as a Certified Information Systems Auditor by the Information Systems Audit and Control Association, among other credentials.

Ephraim is currently employed with one of the top accounting firms in the United Kingdom, where he provides assurance services to corporate entities. Also, Ephraim serves as Director of Corporate Governance on the board of HACTRI (a Nigerian literacy organization). Also, he is a board member of the Itchen Sixth Form College in the United Kingdom.

Ephraim is married to Marian Unuigbe and has two children, Daniel Chukwudi and Eseohen Elizabeth.

Acknowledgement

To my wife, Marian who was just as integral to the book being completed as I was. She was as indispensable to this book's success as I was.

My most important companion, counselor, helper, intercessor, advocate, strengthener, and standby, the Holy Spirit. Thank you.

Other Books by the Author to date

- Succeeding in your career - A Roadmap for Graduates & Young Professionals

- Let's talk about money - A guide to Personal Finances for Young Adults

- How to choose a career path - A Spiritual Perspective to Career Choice & Life.

- The Derailing Youth - For Career Professionals with young adults aged 12 to 19 with absent fathers.

All available on amazon.com and ephraim-unuigbe.online

Contact the author via info@ephraim-unuigbe.online

SERVICES WE OFFER

Career Counselling

We assist individuals of all ages in the clarity and attainment of their career goals, and we also teach students the development of learner-centered skills they can utilize in their academic career and life beyond.

Personal Finance Coaching

Personal finance refers to how well people adhere to a budget when managing their finances. Over time, the goal is to save money, while also spending money on resources that are needed and allocating a particular amount for each living expense. With my guidance, you will learn how to make, manage, and multiply your money.

CV Review and Writing

The modern world of employment demands that your CV stands out, and we provide a range of services through which our professional CV writers can create the CV just for you. Every CV we create is tailored specifically to meet your needs.

Cover Letter and Personal Statement

We will provide you with a professional who knows how to write you a high-performing letter for your job application or personal statement. Paired with our professionally written CV you can differentiate yourself from other applicants.

LinkedIn Profile Optimisation
You can take your LinkedIn profile to the next level and turn it into a powerful career tool that highlights your abilities, experiences, and impresses your network of contacts.

Interview Coaching
Our professionals help you be the best candidate your potential employer has ever seen. A well-rounded approach that addresses the verbal and non-verbal factors.

www.ingramcontent.com/pod-product-compliance
Lightning Source LLC
Chambersburg PA
CBHW070242220526
45465CB00004B/1494